NATIONAL
GEOGRAPHIC

PATHFINDER EDITION

By Terri L. Jones and Susan Blackaby

CONTENTS

Thinking Tall. *In this painting, the artist imagines a city in the future with tall buildings and sleek skyways.*

Back to the

FUTURE

BY TERRI L. JONES

Does your family have a robot that cooks and cleans? Does your mom fly to work with a jetpack on her back? In the 1950s, that's how some people imagined life in the twenty-first century. After all, anything is possible in the future.

What will the future bring?

People just can't stop asking that question. Some bold thinkers try answering it, too. To imagine life in the future, you have to know what might be possible. You also need a lot of imagination.

Science fiction is one way to predict the future. Science fiction, or "sci-fi," is a form of storytelling that blends real science with fantasy. Over the years, science fiction writers, artists, and engineers have had many ideas about what life would be like in the **twenty-first century**. Does your everyday life look anything like what they imagined?

Home, Sweet Robot

In a 1950 book called *The Martian Chronicles*, author Ray Bradbury describes a house that talks. From inside the walls, a voice tells people when to get out of bed, how to dress, and even whose birthday it is.

In Bradbury's remarkable house of the future, there is a robot for every chore. One robot cooks, while other robots set the table and wash the dishes. Meanwhile, tiny mice-like robots scurry around vacuuming the floor.

What's even more remarkable is that some of Bradbury's **predictions** came true. Today, robots are on the job in many places. They vacuum floors, prepare food, build cars, and even explore outer space.

Bradbury wasn't the only one to imagine a house of the future. In the 1950s, Disneyland created a theme park called Tomorrowland. There, visitors toured a futuristic "smart" house, which practically ran itself.

Today, many homes have systems similar to the ones that Tomorrowland **envisioned**, including automatic air temperature controls, sound systems, and microwave ovens that cook meals in just minutes.

Cities in Space

Some predictions that were made in the 1950s were "out of this world." Writers, scientists, and artists imagined huge, bustling cities in space. Some thought that by the early 1990s, Earthlings would live on the moon. Can you imagine sitting under a big lunar dome of glass, watching Earth rise and set?

How would people grow fresh fruits and vegetables in space? Simple. They'd use hydroponics, which is a proven way to grow plants without soil. How would they heat their buildings? Energy from the sun would supply all their power.

Clearly, some of their ideas weren't so crazy. Today, many homes on Earth use solar power. Some experimental cars and planes even run on energy from the sun. While humans do not yet inhabit the moon, astronauts live for months on the International Space Station.

Still, do you know anyone who lives on another planet? Probably not. Some people dream about living on Mars, but the space city of people's imagination is still many years away.

Present + Possible = Future

The dreamers of the 1950s also tried to anticipate how people of the future would communicate. One idea turned up in the "Dick Tracy" comic strip and television show. Tracy was a tough, smart detective who had a very special way of staying in touch with people.

On his wrist, Tracy wore an amazing watch with a telephone that he could use anywhere. The watch also had a two-way television that allowed him to see people while he was talking to them.

The two parts of Tracy's watch—telephone and television—both existed in the 1950s; yet it took an artist to put them together in a whole new way.

Slowly, real life caught up with the comics. Today, people have cell phones with built-in cameras, which allow them to see the person they are calling. People also use webcams to see each other while they talk over the Internet. As "Dick Tracy" predicted, pieces of what was the present came together later, in the future.

Moon Makeover. *This shows how an artist imagined a city on the moon. Can you see the "Earthrise"?*

Rev It Up. *People once thought that in the future jetpacks would be used for everyday travel.*

Up, Up, But Not Away

Some people don't stop at imagining the future; they start building it. That happened when people wanted better forms of transportation. They made models of machines that would **revolutionize** the way we get around, or so they thought.

Take the jetpack, for example. It's a backpack that carries a small rocket engine. You put it on, rev it up, and soar. No need to ask for a ride to school or wait for the bus. That was the idea, anyway. Real life turned out to be a bit more complicated. Doesn't it always?

For starters, jetpacks couldn't carry much fuel, so the average trip was maybe half a minute. As you can imagine, you can't get very far in half a minute.

Then there were problems with safety. Jetpack fuel can heat up to about 700° Celsius (1300° Fahrenheit), making it very dangerous, not to mention flammable. A jetpack's roaring engine can also damage your hearing.

Of course, there are some incredible problem solvers in this world. Someday, a clever inventor may come up with a jetpack that truly takes off. It may be a while, though, so you better hold on to your bus pass.

Getting From Here to There

Another invention that flew was the Aerocar, a flying car with folding wings. A silly idea, right? But wait! An Aerocar was built in 1949, and six more were built over the next ten years. They really worked! Still, the idea never caught on. Maybe that's because Aerocars were too hard to land in the driveway.

How about getting rid of cars altogether? In one science fiction story, people jumped onto moving belts to get around. In the 1950s, that may have sounded crazy, but today, you can see "people movers," escalators, and moving sidewalks in airports, stores, and even on the street.

What people really wanted was an automated "smart car." In the 1950s, car companies tried to manufacture such a vehicle. The idea was for nobody to have to sit behind the wheel. Instead, someone would just push a few buttons and then sit back while the car drove itself. Is such a car possible? Well, you can buy a simpler version today, but it will be a while before a totally automated car is invented and hits the streets.

Super Huge Computer. *In the 1950s, computers were so large that just one filled up an entire room!*

Fast Forward

It's hard to think of a world without computers, but in 1950, only a few computers existed. They were very large—the size of a room. Few people imagined that small, personal computers would become as widespread as they are today.

Then scientists invented the integrated circuit, otherwise known as a computer chip. The chips made computers smaller, which made it possible to do many things with them, including sell them to large numbers of people. Of course, there are now millions of computers in the world.

The future of the 1950s has arrived. Welcome to the twenty-first century! Now think about *your* future and start dreaming. Will you invent the perfect jetpack and make millions? Will you download digital books straight into your brain? Invisibility suits and underwater cities are just two things that may be possible, but what else? Think amazing; think fantastic! The future is yours to invent.

Wordwise

envision: to picture something in your mind

prediction: statement about what someone thinks might happen in the future

revolutionize: to change something a lot or completely

science fiction: storytelling that combines science with made-up events

twenty-first century: between 2001–2100 C.E.

PEDAL POWER

By Susan Blackaby

What is the quickest, easiest, coolest way to get from one place to another? A billion bike riders think they have the answer.

No matter where you look, bicyclists are on the go. In large cities, they pedal to offices. In small towns, they ride to schools. They pump up steep hills and skid over wooded trails. They zoom for fun and zip for work.

People like bikes for many reasons. They're handy and fairly cheap. Even better, bikes are easy to use. Learning to ride a bike only takes about a week. But it took many years to design the modern bikes we see today.

Bumpy Beginnings

In the early 1800s, some people rode bikes called "hobbyhorses." These bikes didn't have pedals, so riders scooted forward by pushing their feet along the ground. Coasting downhill was a breeze, but on flat ground or up hills, it wasn't much different from walking! As you might guess, hobbyhorses were not popular for very long.

Around 1860, bike builders discovered that adding pedals could make the ride more enjoyable. The new bikes were far from perfect, though. On cobblestone streets, the wooden bikes bumped and bounced back and forth, earning them the nickname of "boneshakers."

Bike designers kept rolling forward, trying out new ideas. The "high-wheeler" was the first metal bike.

High-wheelers had huge front wheels— about 1.5 meters (5 feet) tall—but tiny back wheels. Metal spokes in the wheels absorbed the shock from bumps on a rough road. The rider balanced high off the ground and steered very carefully to avoid crashing over headfirst!

Safe Arrival

As people learned new ways to work with metal, bike designs improved. Designers added chains and gears, which allowed riders to change speed more easily and use less pedaling energy. They made the wheels the same size and added rubber tires, too. These **innovations** gave a smooth, safe ride with fewer crash landings. This is considered the birth of the modern bicycle.

Making Progress

In the 1890s, pedal pushing caught on and became a favorite pastime. Fashion designers invented clothing styles that made pedaling more comfortable for women. When workers paved over cobblestone roads, bicyclists could travel more smoothly.

Bikes also inspired some other important inventions. The Wright brothers used bike parts to design their first flying machine in 1903, and Henry Ford used them to make his first car. These two inventions would soon change the world.

Pedal Pushing. Hobbyhorses (near right) had no pedals. Riders moved by pushing their feet along the ground. Boneshakers (far right) were the first bikes with pedals.

Cruisers and Classics

After the invention of cars, the popularity of bikes crashed. Many adults started driving—and stopped pedaling. Bike sales dropped, so bike makers had to come up with a new plan. They created new designs, just for kids.

Flashy cars and motorcycles of the 1930s inspired exciting new bike designs. Bikes called Cruisers had rubber "balloon" tires that were wide and squishy. They rolled right over bumps and dips.

Bikes called Classics were decked out with chrome and fenders, lights, bells, and streamers. They were sturdy and heavy, and could take a lot of punishment from the kids who rode them.

Stunts and Speed

In the 1960s, California kids started a **trend**. They pieced together bike parts to create the "high-rise." It had tall, V-shaped handlebars and banana-shaped seats. On these bikes, kids cruised their neighborhoods "popping wheelies" and performing other stunts.

Stunt bikes were also used for Bicycle Motocross racing, or BMX. Contestants in these events did crazy mid-air tricks and raced over rugged dirt tracks.

In the 1970s, people started worrying about the environment. Cars were polluting the air, and gas was expensive. Bikes provided clean rides and saved money, so adults joined the kids' craze and climbed onto bike seats again.

A new design called the ten-speed was an instant success. The extra gears made pedaling uphill easier. Bikes like these zoom up and down hills and fly around corners in races like the Tour de France.

To the Hills and Beyond

Tooling along smooth roads might be fine for some people, but by the 1980s, a new group of riders wanted to head for the hills. They built mountain bikes to get them there.

The first mountain bikes were made from old, beat-up Classics and Cruisers. Soon, bike makers **refined** these designs and came up with bikes perfectly suited for riders who wanted adventure.

Some skilled mountain bikers do crazy things that no one else should try. They strap on helmets and barrel downhill at high speeds. They go for teeth-jarring rides, bumping over sharp rocks and ragged roots. A rider like this needs a bike strong enough to take a beating.

Other mountain bikers ride for the scenery. They want to follow trails, exploring deep canyons and climbing tall peaks. They need bikes that aren't too heavy to pedal up steep hills and have strong frames.

Today, bike makers continue to improve their designs, making hi-tech bikes more comfortable to ride than ever. From BMX and mountain bikes to ten-speeds and racers, there is a bike to fit every occasion. There is even a bike you ride sideways; you face sideways but move forward, as if you were snowboarding. A fold-up bike can slide under a desk, while an electronic bike can give your legs a rest.

Now think: What totally new kind of bike could *you* design? What cool idea do you have that will keep bike designs pedaling into the future? Start thinking, and enjoy the ride!

Bikes ACROSS TIME

Hobbyhorse	Boneshaker	High-wheeler
Early 1800s	*1860s*	*1870s*

Bikes and Balance. *On a high-wheeler bike, the rider perched on a seat about 1.5 meters (5 feet) above the ground.*

Modern Racers. *Today's streamlined designs let bike riders go faster than ever!*

WORD WISE

innovation: a new thing, idea, or way of doing something

refine: to improve something by making small changes to it

trend: something that becomes very popular

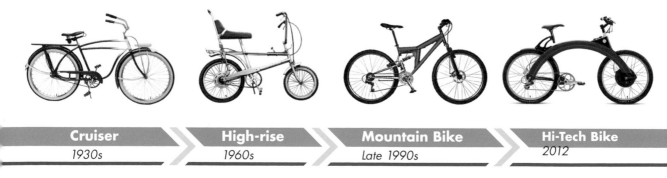

Cruiser	High-rise	Mountain Bike	Hi-Tech Bike
1930s	1960s	Late 1990s	2012

THE FUTURE IS NOW

Fast-forward to the future and then answer these questions.

1 Describe three predictions from the 1950s about life in the future.

2 What twenty-first century invention did people not predict in the 1950s?

3 Why did bike makers create Cruisers and Classic bicycles?

4 How are today's bicycles similar to bikes from the 1800s? How are they different?

5 How is information organized in "Present + Possible = Future" and "Bikes Across Time"?

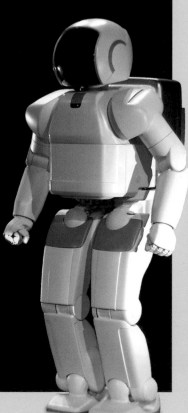